ISFP:

Understand And Break Free
From Your Own Limitations

MATTHEW BRIGHTHOUSE

Table of Contents

Introduction

Learning about your personality is a rewarding and fulfilling journey to go on. You begin to understand yourself much better, you identify where your strong points are, celebrating them, and you also learn to understand your weak points. Knowing your weaknesses is actually a positive thing because you can turn them on their head, learn to truly pick them apart, and then put into place ways to rid them from your life, or at least minimize their impact. Once you knock these road-blocks down, you can begin towards a new journey, with an end destination that is much more fulfilling than before.

By taking the Myers Briggs personality test, you identify your main personality type. The fact you have picked up this book or downloaded it means that you have probably been identified as the ISFP personality type. You are the Adventurer, you are someone who is creative, someone who is fearless, and someone who has great empathy for others.

Overall, you're a pretty great guy or gal!

Of course, nobody is perfect, so you also have downsides too. By embarking on this personality test, you have given yourself the opportunity to understand what your upsides and downsides are. This means you can minimize their impact on your life, and that of others, and cast aside any limitations that are holding you back in what you want to achieve.

The point of this book is to help you analyze your personality type, so you can understand yourself much better. You will be able to see why you react the way you do in certain situations, you will be able to see yourself in so many of the examples we give, and you will also learn to celebrate the strong points that we will allude to several times over! We are also going to talk about your personality type's common weaknesses too. Now, it's important to realize that nothing in this book is meant as a criticism, it is merely a tool to help you improve and cast aside any problems which are caused by the common weaknesses of your ISFP personality type. And with some new awareness, you will be able to grow into a better version of yourself.

Every single type in the spectrum has strengths and weaknesses because that is what makes us human. Whilst we can never realistically expect to cast aside every single weakness we have and make ourselves perfect, we can learn to understand our weaknesses, and also understand how they impact on our lives in a negative way. By doing that, we can turn them on their head and actually turn them into positives. If you don't know what your downsides are, you can't work on them!

This journey is going to be a true journey of self-discovery, but it's also important to note that nobody is ever 100% one particular personality type. It's a good idea to read about all of the types, because not only will that help you understand other people, who are different types to you, but it will also help you to see where you might have traits in other camps too. Aside from anything else, it's actually really interesting to learn about people and what makes them tick. If you are a manager, or you're thinking of heading into that line of work, then understanding the different personality types in the spectrum can help you with your people management skills.

There is never anything negative involved in learning about what makes us tick, and the most valuable journey you will ever go on involves learning about yourself at your very core.

So, buckle your seatbelt, hold on tight, and allow yourself to be immersed in a world of the ISFP personality.

1
The Fine Line Between Strength and Weakness

What kind of job do you do? Do you have a creative kind of job? If not, do you find yourself yearning for a change, eager to do something which piques your curiosity and your imagination? Do you have a creative hobby that you enjoy in your spare time? Do you wish you had more time to dedicate to that hobby?

If you're nodding your head then you are a true ISFP!

As we have mentioned already, by taking the Myers Briggs personality test you have identified yourself as an ISFP type. You are therefore known as the Adventurer – how exciting! You are a true enigma in so many ways, yet your emotions and your empathic nature really rule your life to so many different degrees. You are kind-hearted, generous, and you really 'feel' people, yet you also find it difficult to open up and let people see the real you. You are strong, yet you are soft.

As we said, a true enigma!

Throughout this book, we are going to give you real and practical advice on how to maximize the plus points of your personality type, and also how to minimize the negative effects that your weaknesses may have. Don't worry, we all have downsides, it's part of being human, but the key is to know what they are and to tackle them head-on, rather than allowing them to place roadblocks in the way of your life and the things you want to achieve.

So, you're an ISFP, but what does that really stand for and mean?

Let's explore.

ISFP stands for:

I = Introversion
S = Sensing
F = Feeling
P = Perceiving

That is how the Myers Briggs personality test classifies your particular type. That doesn't mean anything to you at this point, however, so let's delve a little deeper.

Introversion
You are a quiet soul, someone who listens and watches, rather than someone who speaks. That doesn't mean you are a wallflower, however, because you're a 'cool' kind of dude or dudette! Your quietness isn't because you fear being heard or that you don't want to be seen, it is that you would rather save your voice and your presence for the things in your life that really matter and mean something to you. You observe the world, and you take on board what you need to see from that observation.

Ironically, this quiet nature is also down to the fact that you are ruled by your emotions. A little later in the book, we are going to talk about how you can rein in your emotional structure just a little, to make your life easier overall, but on the upside, your emotions also make you a hugely empathic person. Your creativity also stems from your emotions, because it is an outlet for the way you feel.

ISFPs are cool and edgy, and they would rather listen and stand on the sides lines, observing the scene, than be in the middle of it. One very famous celebrity ISFP was the late, great Michael Jackson. Jackson performed with an imaginary mask on, rather than being a true 'out there' personality in his own right when he was on stage. If you knew anything about MJ when he wasn't on stage, you'll know he was quiet, someone who preferred to speak through his creative art.

Sensing
Working a little against introversion, ISFPs don't tend to use their intuition when dealing with people and situations as much as they use their logic. For an emotional personality type, this is quite strange, but it's an interesting mix all the same! Your ability to watch and understand what is going on under the surface means that you can make effective decisions on issues that really matter. Having said that, you sense using your emotions too. You are very connected to other people through their feelings, and this is something we're going to talk about in greater detail later on.

Sensing versus intuition is the way in which we deal with situations and process the data that comes our way. Whilst you don't tend to rely on intuition at all times, you can call upon it when you need to. Learning to listen to and trust your intuition is something you can work on. When you combine logic and intuition, you can make some truly 'bang on' decisions!

Feeling

In total contradiction to the 'sensing' part of your personality makeup, ISFPs throw the rule book out of the window here! You feel rather than think when you are understanding a situation. Whereas in our last letter we talked about how you react and process data, feeling means that you are ruled by your emotions in all other aspects of your life. This is a good thing in many ways, but it can also be a hindrance too, as you can allow your emotions to boil over and get you into a little trouble from time to time! We are going to address this potential issue in a later chapter, to allow you to understand how to maximize your emotions for good, but also rein them in when they threaten to cause you issues.

Perceiving

The opposite of perceiving is judgment, so this means you are not a judgemental person – good news! You can understand that people are different, deal with situations in different ways and that we are all very individual in our own right. You could never be accused of being narrow-minded, and your creative mind means that you can see solutions to problems which others probably can't. You are also someone who is quite perceptive in terms of what other people are feeling too. You could be described as an empath to some degree, although it is more likely that you simply can tell when someone is down, or having trouble with a situation in their life. This is a strength you can work on, even more, to make it a true asset in your life, and for others too. Again, we'll address this in more detail later on.

Now we know what the letters actually stand for, we can see the basis of your personality, and build on our journey from there.

So, we've talked about the fact that every personality type has strengths and weaknesses. This very fact makes us human beings. It should never be your aim to be perfect, i.e. to eradicate your weaknesses completely, because that's simply not realistic. A perfect person is not an interesting person, they are not someone you want to spend time with! A perfect person basically doesn't exist either. What you should be aiming for is to identify the weaknesses you think are putting limitations and walls in the way of what you want to achieve in life, as well as stopping you from attracting opportunities that could lead you down very favorable roads.

In order to do this, however, we need to know what said strengths and weaknesses are. Let's start with your strengths.

ISFP Strengths

- **A laid-back, what will be will be attitude**
  As an ISFP, you don't tend to stress and worry about the things you can't change or control. This is a great strength to have because becoming overwhelmed in a world of overthinking is not a great way to live. The ability to simply take life as it comes is a great

asset to your personality type, and ironically, it also helps you in your many creative endeavors too.

- **Charming**
  ISFPs are introverted, but they are also very charming too. If an ISFP shows you attention, you feel special! You have that charming power over people, and you can easily draw them in, as they become fascinated with your laid back, artistic vibe. It is important not to use this for negatives, however!

- **Empathic and sensitive to the feelings of other people**
  You are very good at picking up when someone around you is upset or struggling with a particular issue. If you've ever heard of an empath, there is a good chance that you may be one with your personality type, but even if not, you are simply very sensitive. This can sometimes lead you to feel overwhelmed with a range of emotions, as you pick up on whatever someone else is feeling, but it also puts you in a great position to help out too. This is something you can develop and work on.

- **Creative and imaginative minds**
  You are likely to be involved in some kind of artistic endeavor, be it painting, writing, drawing, singing, dancing, basically anything which involves using your imagination and your creative wares. If you can find a job to pour all of that imagination into, you'll not only be very successful, but you will be very fulfilled on a personal level too.

- **Very passionate, and will see things through to the end**

With that creative streaks comes a very passionate nature, and you are not someone who will give up on something they truly believe in. This passion can occasionally spill over into anger when you don't feel that you are being given the credit you deserve, and this is also something to work on from time to time. You are a great person to have on the team with the desire to finish things off, where many others simply start something and never finish.

ISFP Weaknesses

- **Very independent, and can often feel 'boxed in'**
  Whilst being independent is certainly not a negative, an ISFP does have a tendency to take this to rather fierce levels, leaving them feeling 'boxed in' or oppressed, when there really isn't a need to be. This is probably all down to that creative mind, a need to be out there doing something, exploring something, changing something. Independence should never be changed, but perhaps understanding that on occasion routine has to occur, in order for life to achieve balance, is something to think about.

- **Not a big future planner**
  As an ISFP, you are quite unpredictable, and that means that you don't really like to plan ahead. We mentioned in our strengths section that you don't worry about things you can't control or change, but the flipside of that is that you sometimes have a problem planning anything or committing to anything! This can be frustrating for those around you, especially if we are talking about romantic relationships. Understanding that there are some

benefits to planning certain things, just a little, will
serve you well.

- **Ruled by emotions**
  We talked about 'living in the moment', but again the
  downside is that you are often ruled by your
  emotions. This can also lead you to being consumed
  by them when you allow them to really get a hold of
  your day. Learning to rein in your emotions and
  control them a little will allow you to achieve a more
  harmonious balance in your life, and will knock
  down a great big barrier you might have been putting
  in the way of achieving something important. This is
  an issue we will dedicate a chapter to later in the
  book.

- **Allows criticism to affect self-esteem**
  As an ISFP, you are very affected by emotions, as we
  mentioned, but that also means that you can take
  criticism to heart a little too easily. This can bring
  down your self-esteem and cause confidence issues.
  We are going to address this weakness in a later
  chapter because confidence is vital to a happy and
  successful life. If you can learn to understand that
  not every comment made is a criticism in a negative
  way, you will be able to accept the opinions of others
  as just that, opinion, not fact.

Now we know the key strengths and weaknesses of
the ISFP personality type, we can begin our journey.
Remember, nothing in this book is meant in a
negative way, and everything is designed to help you
become the best you can be! You may be putting
walls in the way of success and progression without
even realizing it, and the aim of this book is to help

you knock down those walls and the things that are causing you to put them there in the first place.

So, without further ado, let's begin our journey into the wonderful world of the ISFP personality type.

2
Learn to Embrace The Future

One of the main weaknesses we mentioned in terms of the ISFP personality type, is a lack of planning for the future, and a lack of commitment in many different areas of life. Many people suffer from this so-called affliction, whether that is through a fear of being 'tied down', or simply because they don't like to think past today because they have no clue what is going to happen. As an ISFP, you are somewhere in the middle.

It's not that you are terrified of making plans, because you're as fearless as the next person, but you simply don't see the point. You live in the moment, living for today, and you don't like to feel that you are 'boxed in' in any way.

This is a good thing and a bad thing all rolled into one.

Firstly, let's talk about the positive. It's great that you don't worry about the future, it's great that you have that 'Hakuna Matata' mantra to your life. Let's be honest, more people should have this carefree nature, especially when you think about how easy it is to become stressed out these days. Stress can cause very serious health issues and can be a precursor to depression and anxiety. That is not a road to be voluntarily going down, and as an ISFP, you're not really someone who is likely to head in that direction easily. This is all down to that 'live for today' mindset you have.

It's likely that a lot of people look towards your way of life with envy, because having a 'whatever will be will be' way of thinking is a great trait. On the flipside, however, it's likely that your significant other is a little frustrated by your lack of future planning!

We can joke about it to a degree, but the fact remains that if you really refuse to commit to a future plan when you are in a romantic relationship with someone, the chances are that they could become frustrated and possibly decide to leave. This wouldn't be because they don't love and care for you, but it would be that they simply can't commit themselves to a person who won't commit to them.

Now, you will no doubt have any idea this is happening. It's not that you don't want to commit, it's that you simply don't see why you have to make a big song and dance about it – live for today!

Can you see where we're going with this?

Misunderstandings have wrecked many a relationship in the past, perhaps in your past, so it is something to be aware of.

As you can see, this lack of future planning has an upside and a downside. The key to managing this weakness is to find the fine line between going too far in one direction and losing that very enviable trait of living in the moment, yet also knowing when to make commitments and plans. It's not as complicated as it sounds!

Commitment And Planning Isn't a Prison

This particular issue all comes down to the fact that an ISFP personality type needs freedom. It's likely that you don't like to feel like you're trapped or boxed into a decision, you like to feel able to move in any direction, at any given time. You may see planning or commitment as a way of nailing you down, but it's really not the case. Therefore, the key to changing the limitations you might be placing in the way of progression is to change the way you see commitment and planning.

For instance, do you see making a commitment as a wonderful thing? Something to give you security and safety, or do you see it as a limitation to stop you doing what you want?

Many people who are scared of commitment think about it in the wrong way. Commitment isn't about being locked in a room, robbed of freedom, it's about a plan, something to work towards, something to give you security, and something to help you grow and move in a different direction.

If you can change your mindset towards planning and commitment from the negative to the positive, you will instantly see a change in how you feel about it.

The best way to think about planning and commitment is this – both offer you a route towards new possibilities, possibilities that may bring you everything you ever dreamed of!

If you don't have a plan, it's unlikely that your dream will ever come true. Life isn't just going to drop whatever you want into your lap, you need to have a plan in order to make it happen, you need to know what to do and how to do it. You don't have set yourself rigid plans, just goals; this is a vague direction in which to go, nothing to tie you down, nothing to make you feel like you are in a prison, and nothing which is set in stone. Consider your plans as guidelines.

Something that you may find useful is to think about your ideal life (your vision). Then think about your purpose (your why). With those 2 things carefully thought out, you can then create plans and goals to direct you towards your heart's desire.

3
Learn to Harness Your Emotions

In our first chapter, we talked about the fact that your personality type is controlled to a large degree by your emotions. Emotions can, as we all know, be negative and positive. The key to understanding your emotions is knowing where they are coming from, what they are attached to, and whether they are rooted in fear, or something more substantial.

Now, ISFPs are not at the total mercy of their feelings and the changing tide of their emotions, but they are to a larger degree than more logical types. This can leave you feeling up one minute, and down the next, which can cause you problems in your daily life if you allow your emotions to really get under your skin.

Now, there is a trick here, and it is one which will really help you maximize your potential in life – learn how to control your emotions, and they will no longer be able to control you. It's all about mindset training, and whilst it will take some work at first, after a while, it will become second nature. Be patient here, because the end result is more than worth it.

- **What are your triggers?** – What triggers your emotions? It is a memory, is it words by someone you love or trust, it is criticism? If you can understand what causes your emotions to peak, then you can put into action steps to help minimize the effect it has on you. You might also notice a pattern, e.g. it is the same thing which causes you to feel this way, or maybe even the same person. Perhaps keep an emotional diary for a week or so, and see if you can identify any patterns or triggers you might not be aware of.

- **Are you seeing things clearly?** – Are you allowing your emotions to cloud your judgment, and after a while you see things more realistically? This is often the case, and after a while, when you have calmed down, you will probably see that the situation or issue isn't as bad as you thought. Learning to take a breath and stay in the moment (something you should be able to grasp as an ISFP) will help you tenfold. When you feel those emotions beginning to rise, be it upset, anger, sadness, or something else, close your eyes, take a deep breath or two, count to ten, and refocus. This should be enough to restore clarity.

- **Think about meditation** – No, it's not an 'out there' idea, it actually works. Meditation is a great way to bringing your mind towards the clearer side and controlling those emotions that may otherwise threaten to run away with you. You don't have to sit there for hours on end lost in a trance, you can simply dedicate 15 minutes in the morning before work, or perhaps before bed, to realigning your thoughts, and keeping those emotions firmly under control.

These three suggestions are easy to implement, and they will all have a huge impact on how well you can grab back some control over your emotions.

It's often the case that someone who is creative and imaginative is very in touch with their emotions, and this is something you don't want to lose. Emotions make us human; they make the good times amazing, and the bad time's something to learn from. Whilst emotions can sometimes feel overwhelming, it's important never to lose sight of the fact that feeling is a good thing, and that not feeling is, well, a cold and boring way to live your life.

Because your emotions are intrinsically linked to your creativity, it's vital that you find a balance in your life that you can control and pull back whenever you need to. We mentioned that you are someone who lives in the moment, and whilst that is a great asset, it is also a downside in terms of emotions because it means you are fully 'in' the emotion, rather than just skimming over it. If you can learn to understand what the emotion is, keep it in perspective, and handle it, then you can still live in the moment (as you always should) and be level-headed at the same time.

It can be done, but it is going to take some time at first. Remember though, never let yourself become unemotional – being emotional is a gift, it is something which takes strength, and you can control your emotions, they do not control you. Write this down and repeat it as a mantra every morning, or whenever you start to feel overwhelmed – you are in control. Firmly.

4

Learn to Not Allow Criticism to Dampen Your Self-Esteem

Our next chapter runs on seamlessly from the chat we just had about emotions. Whilst you are very emotional when in the moment, it is possible to gain control. You have the tools to do that now you have read through our last chapter. Now we need to address the effect that criticism has on your self-esteem.

You are creative, you love to express yourself through an art form, but that does, unfortunately, open you up to criticism from others who are less artistically minded. It also opens you up to criticism on your actual art form too. This is par for the course – criticism is part of life, especially in the artistic world. However, is it really criticism that you are experiencing, or is it just someone's opinion?

ISFP's can sometimes allow criticism to upset them because they take the comment to heart. This can lead to self-esteem being knocked, because they start to believe the comment.

You are sensitive to other people and their feelings, but your own feelings are sensitive too, especially when it comes to your creative art. You want to be liked, of course, we all do. And you want others to like the creative wares that you are expressing and showing. If someone else doesn't like them, you take it very personally.

Now, is that person's comment an opinion or a fact?

If someone doesn't like a painting you have done, for example, is it a fact that it is no good? Or, more likely, is it someone's opinion?

We are all programmed to like different things, dislike different things, and feel a different way about everything in life. If we all liked the same things, life would be boring, and can you imagine the chaos in terms of finding a life partner? We'd all want the same person! Variety is the spice of life, and that means that you really cannot please everyone you come across.

The key to overcoming this particular limitation is in understanding and accepting that very fact.

For instance, do you like jazz music? Perhaps you do, perhaps you don't, but does every single person on the planet like jazz music? No! Does that mean that jazz music is rubbish and shouldn't be allowed to be played ever again? Of course not! Millions of people love jazz music, millions of people hate it, and millions of people have no opinion whatsoever.

Can you see where we're going with this?

Opinion is just that – one person's thoughts on something. That one person might not like something you have done, but the next person might love it, and a thousand people after them. It's important not to focus on that one negative remark, and instead focus on the thousand good ones!

Unfortunately, as human beings, we tend to focus on the negatives before the positives – this seems to be part of our DNA and our human make-up. Our brains are hard-wired to recognize that negative first, and it takes some work to change that mindset and make your brain first recognize the positive. Once you see the positive, the negative pales into insignificance, and that is what you need to learn how to do.

Let's get positive, this can be done!

- The next time someone says something negative to you, e.g. they don't like your new hairstyle, accept the comment. Acknowledge it with a shrug.
- Now, ask yourself if that person is really that important to you. Do you really care what they think? Maybe you do, maybe you don't, but do you like every single thing about that person too? Probably not! The difference is that you don't go and tell them what you don't like, whereas they did. Their karma, not yours.
- Next, think about the remark, and ask yourself if you have received any positive remarks about the same matter. For instance, did anyone compliment you on your hairstyle?
- Ask yourself why you are listening to the negative, but you didn't pay any attention to the positive. It makes no sense, right? Once you begin thinking in

this way, you will notice that it really is just an opinion and not a fact.

Once you begin analyzing these comments in this way you will be able to understand that negative remarks are not fact, they are opinion, and we are all entitled to our own individual opinions. We are made of sugar and spice, sweet and sour, and that means we are all individually different, and wonderful in our own right.

Criticism Can Be Constructive

It's important to realize that not all criticism is something to shrug off and ignore, because some of it can actually be very useful indeed. For instance, a comment about a song you have written; this could either be an opinion that you don't need to listen to because it's based on jealousy or nothing particularly substantial (some people do this), or it could be a comment that could actually be taken on board and used to improve. Some criticism is ideal for learning.

Let's continue with the songwriting example. If someone mentions that a line you have written in the song doesn't make much sense, think about it. Are they right? Say they give you an idea for a replacement, a different route to take the song down. Listen to what they're saying, are they onto something? You could then take that idea and redesign your song, to improve it tenfold. If you hadn't listened to that comment and analyzed it in a positive way, you would never have had the opportunity to change your song into something even more wonderful!

As you can see, some criticism can actually be useful, a tool for learning and improvement. It isn't meant as a negative dig at you, and it's nothing personal, it can actually be genuinely intended to help you out. Knowing the difference between someone who is simply giving you a negative comment for the hell of it (because they may be jealous or simply having a bad day), and someone who is trying to help you out, is key.

As you learn to take things less personally, using the methods we have talked about above, you will see the difference between the two situations much more clearly.

5
Learn to Rein in Your 'Risky' Side

As an ISFP, you're certainly not a boring person to be around! You might be introverted and prefer to stay on the sidelines, but that doesn't mean you're a wallflower or boring in any way, you simply save your vigor and excitement for those who matter!

You are impulsive and you are spontaneous, you live in the moment, and you make decisions on the fly.

Is this good? Of course it is! However, everything in life has a flipside, and the flipside of this particular personality trait is that you can sometimes be spontaneous on the route towards riskier types of behavior. We're talking about taking risks that could turn out to be unsafe, gambling, and the like.

The 'live for today' mindset is fantastic, but if you allow it to take you down riskier routes, you could end up losing out, and perhaps even suffering.

There is a fine line between being spontaneous and being careless, and it's important to always tread on the right side of that line. This is all about being mindful of your decisions and taking a second to ask yourself whether it's a good idea or not, before you shrug your shoulders and go for it anyway, most probably!

Follow this thought process:

- What is the action you're considering? Break it down into a simplistic explanation
- What are the potential gains? What good things may come of it? Be realistic here
- What are the potential losses? What bad things may realistically come of it?
- Does the loss make the gain worth it? Again, realism is key here

It is likely that by taking a few seconds to consider these questions, you'll talk yourself out of anything that is too risky, and the spontaneous urge will disappear. However, if you decide that the action isn't negatively risky, then, by all means, go for it, spontaneity is to be celebrated from time to time!

In the last two chapters we talked about emotions, and this chapter is actually linked to that same subject, although you might not realize it. Your emotions will give you that spontaneous urge; for instance, if you're feeling bored, you might suddenly decide to do something to bring a little excitement to your day. Taking the time out to ask yourself the above questions before making the action a reality will make sure that whatever you're planning on doing to bring that excitement into your life, is safe, sensible, and not at all risky.

It's not about being boring or reining in the fun you have in life, it's about making sure that the fun you have isn't going to have major consequences once the initial buzz is over. We all try and get that buzz occasionally, but there are much better ways to find it than putting yourself in a difficult situation.

For instance, let's consider gambling for a second. You might have never gambled in your life, you might not even agree with it, but it is a good example to talk about.

A little flutter here and there is fine. Most people do it occasionally, whether we're talking about having a go on the lottery at New Year, grabbing a scratch card impulsively when buying a morning newspaper, or making a bet on a big sporting event. These occasional gambling episodes are okay, because they don't involve large amounts of money, and they aren't habitual. A couple of dollars on a scratch card or a bet on a basketball game isn't going to cause you to be unable to pay your rent at the end of the month. It's about thinking realistically and sensibly when weighing up the pros and cons of the action.

Now, it's important to realize that risky behavior often has an addictive side to it. When that addiction grabs hold, it can be very difficult to see sense, and in that situation, it's even more important to ask yourself those questions we listed above.

Of course, we're not suggesting that if you gamble occasionally you're going to become addicted, but it is important to keep the idea in your mind, to keep everything in perspective, and to avoid any potentially damaging situations in your life.

The Extreme Buzz

Another potential area for risky behavior for ISFP's is extreme sports.

We all love a buzz, and extreme sports such as skydiving, bungee jumping, and the likes, are well-known to give that seriously addictive adrenaline rush that we all crave from time to time. Whilst it's fine to indulge occasionally, remember safety should always come first. Always ask yourself if what you're doing is safe, and always take the right precautions. This isn't a lecture, it's common sense!

That need for a buzz high is prevalent in the ISFP personality type more than any other, so understanding that the risks you take need to be safe, secure, and sensible, will save you from potential consequences. As an alternative perhaps learn to find that buzz high in your creative work instead, and you'll not only cut down on the potential risk, but you'll also improve your craft at the same time!

6

Learn How to Use Your Empathy For Greater Good

One of the greatest strengths of the ISFP personality type is the ability to really tune into the feelings of other people. There is a chance you have empathic qualities, but even if you don't believe in that, you are someone who is very sensitive to feelings of others, and this can help you identify when something isn't quite right with a friend or family member.

A self-discovery journey such as this isn't just about minimizing your weaknesses and learning to knock down the limitations that you're placing in front of yourself, it's also about maximizing your strengths for greater good. You have many fantastic qualities as an ISFP, and whilst you're working on your weaknesses and learning how to control them, you should also be learning how to maximize those strong points too. If you've got it, go ahead and flaunt it!

The fact that you are so tuned in to your own emotions means that you can easily recognize emotions in other people, and it may also be that when they are down, you can feel those negative waves washing off of them quite easily. It might also be that those negative waves begin to affect you also, and can work to bring you down too. This is where those potential empathic qualities come into play.

Empaths are able to pick up on the emotions of other people very easily, often without even knowing them. These emotions are almost like an aura to an empath, so whenever someone close to them is happy, they're happy, and whenever someone close to them is sad, they're sad too. If someone close is suffering from a hard time, and they're feeling very down, it can be hard for the empathic person to deal with, because those negative emotions are picked up too, whilst also dealing with whatever they have got going on in their life. Some people who are very emotionally sensitive have also reported finding it hard to be out in large crowds, because there's just too much feeling information coming at them from all angles. For you, it's likely that this isn't the case, but for those closely linked to you, you can certainly tune in quite easily.

The life of an empath can be a difficult one, but it's also a gift in so many ways. If you know someone is hurting, you can help them.

Whether you believe you are an empath or you're simply sensitive, tune into those around you. If you notice that someone is acting a little 'off', and they just seem like they're upset about something, you're picking up a vibe, then try and think if there is something you can do. Do you know them very well? If so, sit them down somewhere relaxed, perhaps over a coffee, and ask if everything is okay. Sometimes, it can be as simple as a person saying 'hey I know you're not okay, talk to me' for them to open up, offload, and then feel better. You have that ability to make someone else feel better, and that's a wonderful thing.

If you don't know them well enough to do this, then you can go about it in a more subtle way. For instance, if it's someone at work, a colleague you know, but you don't know that well, you need to be a little indirect. Small acts of kindness go a long way in situations such as this, so perhaps say 'I'm going to get coffee from Starbucks, do you want one?' – the simple gesture might perk them up just a little. That could also be an 'in' to get to know them better, and who knows, you might find yourself with a new friend. These things all have a snowball effect, and good deeds are rewarded with good things in return.

Being sensitive to the feelings and emotions of others truly is something very special to experience, and although at times it might feel like a burden, embrace it, and use it for the greater good of those around you. You'll be amazed how good it makes you feel too!

7

Learn How to Maximize Your Creativity

We know that as an ISFP you're likely to be a creative kind of person, and whether you do your creative endeavors as a hobby or a job, there are many ways to maximize your potential, and perhaps even make a little cash out of it!

It is generally considered that we are either creative or academic, with a few people falling somewhere in the middle. Creative minds like to work with their hands and their imaginations, and you certainly have a very vivid imagination! Working alongside creativity comes emotions, and we have already talked at length about the fact you have a lot of those in the moment! We talked about learning how to control your emotions so they don't control you, but how about learning how to harness them and turn them into creativity?

If you're feeling a little overwhelmed with an emotion right at that moment, why not do something constructive with it? If your creative talent is to write, grab some paper and write about your emotion, or what is in your head at that time. If you love to draw, why not grab a pencil and get sketching? You get the picture here, in more ways than one.

Basically, emotion is an opportunity here, because it will help you to express what you're feeling, and the creative result will really come from the soul, something really genuine. You will also get that emotion out, and that is the healthiest way to deal with your feelings.

If you really love what you do, then you'll put more time and effort into it, it will be an enjoyable way to spend your time, you'll be able to process what you're feeling and going through much more effectively, and you'll be better at it in the end. So, if your creative talent is something you can make cash from, why not go for it?

There are many freelancing opportunities for creative talents, such as writing, graphic design, illustrations, songwriting, all manner of things which you won't know about until you do a little research. Whilst you might not be able to jump straight into it and make cash out of it, you can work towards that as your final aim. Yes, you don't like planning, we know this because you're an ISFP, but in this case, perhaps a little pre-planning could be an enjoyable experience if it gets you where you really want to be?

Having aims will help you achieve your dreams, and creating an action plan will help you get there. When it comes to your artistic endeavors, you're more tuned in to them than many other personality types; you love to express yourself, and you take great pleasure in presenting your art to other people. Of course, you're not a fan of criticism, but by taking into account the steps we talked about in our earlier chapter on not taking criticism to heart, you'll be able to overcome that step with ease, over time.

Why not go for it?

Of course, if you don't want to make your creative talent a job, then make it a priority in your life as a hobby. Give yourself the time to enjoy it, and pour your heart and soul into it. This is your way of expressing yourself clearly, your way of processing what is going on in your life and in your soul – you owe it to yourself to make it a priority in your life. Enjoy it!

By giving yourself the time, you are maximizing your potential and allowing your creativity to grow.

8
Conclusion

And there we have it, the emotional, creative, and spontaneous world of the ISFP personality type. You are someone who is interesting, an enigma, a creative soul, and a potential empath. You are complicated, but wonderfully so, and you have a world of potential within you, to maximize that creative talent you have, as well as the ability to help other people through your emotional sensitivity.

It is vital that ISFPs continue to keep their creative talent as close to the very core of their daily life as possible. This is for many reasons, but mainly because a) it is a healthy way to express emotion, and b) they're likely to be very talented at whatever they do!

If you're the ISFP, or someone close to you, the advice within this book will be invaluable. Let's assume that you're the ISFP here. What is your talent? Maximize it, spend more time doing it. This is your way of expressing yourself to the world, and you should do that whenever you get the chance.

We have talked about your strengths and we have celebrated them. We have talked about your weaknesses and we have addressed them. Now it is up you to work at your own pace on the advice we have given. It's important to remember that nothing in this book is a criticism of your personality type, it is a line of constructive advice to help you overcome any roadblocks that might be standing in the way of your future success. It's unrealistic to expect to eradicate these from your life, and you shouldn't want to! Your weaknesses are part of your make-up, they are part of what makes you the person you are – we all have flaws, we need them in our lives to balance up the positives. Nobody can be perfect, it's not a realistic aim to have!

With that in mind, we shouldn't totally ignore those weaknesses, because they might be causing us to avoid action in our lives that could bring us huge benefit. We place walls in the way of situations when we're either scared of what is on the other side, or when we lack the self-belief to take the jump towards it. Knocking down those walls, by addressing our weaknesses, can take us to places that we could have only dreamed about before.

Remember that as a human being, you're very unlikely to be 100% any one particular personality type. It's likely that you display traits of other types too, and in order to really complete your true self-discovery journey, you need to know about all of those traits. How do you do that? You read about them all! Its a really interesting subject if nothing else, and you will certainly gain perspective on the reasons that people act the way they do in life, as well as learning how to deal with them in the most effective way.

We hope this book has given you serious food for thought, and that you take our advice and try out a few of the exercises we've mentioned. Your talents as an ISFP are endless, and the future is certainly very bright!

Thank you for purchasing and reading this book. If you enjoyed it or found it useful then I'd really appreciate it if you would post a short review on Amazon. I do read all the reviews personally so that I can continually write what people are wanting.

If you'd like to leave a review then please visit the link below:

https://www.amazon.com/dp/B079L2QP6N

Thanks for your support and good luck!

Check Out My Other Books

Below you'll find some of my other books that are popular on Amazon and Kindle as well. Simply search the titles listed below on Amazon. Alternatively, you can visit my author page on Amazon to see other work done by me.

ENFP: Understand and Break Free From Your Own Limitations

INFP: Understand and Break Free From Your Own Limitations

ENFJ: Understand and Break Free From Your Own Limitations

INFJ: Understand and Break Free From Your Own Limitations

ENFP: INFP: ENFJ: INFJ: Understand and Break Free From Your Own Limitations – The Diplomat Bundle Series

INTP: Understand and Break Free From Your Own Limitations

INTJ: Understand and Break Free From Your Own Limitations

ENTP: Understand and Break Free From Your Own Limitations

ENTJ: Understand and Break Free From Your Own Limitations

<u>ESTJ: Understand and Break Free From Your Own Limitations</u>

<u>ISTJ: Understand and Break Free From Your Own Limitations</u>

<u>ISFJ: Understand and Break Free From Your Own Limitations</u>

<u>ESFJ: Understand and Break Free From Your Own Limitations</u>

<u>OPTION B: F**K IT - How to Finally Take Control Of Your Life And Break Free From All Expectations. Live A Limitless, Fearless, Purpose Driven Life With Ultimate Freedom</u>

www.ingramcontent.com/pod-product-compliance
Lightning Source LLC
Chambersburg PA
CBHW051402250726
48656CB00006B/2231